# EXTREME SCIENTISTS

# EXTREME SCIENTISTS

## EXPLORING NATURE'S MYSTERIES FROM PERILOUS PLACES

BY DONNA M. JACKSON

HOUGHTON MIFFLIN HARCOURT
BOSTON  NEW YORK

**To bold spirits:
including my sister, Susan,
who bravely battles MS,
and in memory of Maggie**

All rights reserved. Originally published in hardcover in the United States
by Houghton Mifflin Harcourt Publishing Company, 2009.

For information about permission to reproduce selections from this book,
write to Permissions, Houghton Mifflin Harcourt Publishing Company,
215 Park Avenue South, New York, New York 10003.

www.hmhco.com

The text of this book is set in Minion.
Photo credits appear on page 79.

The Library of Congress has cataloged the hardcover edition as follows:
Jackson, Donna M., 1959–
Extreme scientists: exploring nature's mysteries from perilous places/by
Donna M. Jackson.
p. cm.—(Scientists in the Field)
1. Science—Vocational guidance—Juvenile literature. 2. Explorers—Juvenile
literature. 3. Science—Juvenile literature. I. Title.
Q147.J33  2009
509.2'2—dc22
2008036796

ISBN: 978-0-618-77706-8 hardcover
ISBN: 978-0-544-25003-1 paperback

Manufactured in China
SCP 10.9 8 7 6 5 4 3 2 1

4500462973

# ACKNOWLEDGMENTS

Many thanks to the scientists and others who took time to share their pioneering pursuits and images for the book—it's an honor to share your stories and photos with readers: Paul Flaherty, meteorologist and flight director, National Oceanic and Atmospheric Administration (NOAA) hurricane hunters; Hazel Barton, Ph.D., Ashland Endowed Professor of Integrative Science and assistant professor of biological sciences at Northern Kentucky University; Stephen Sillett, Ph.D., Kenneth L. Fisher Chair in Redwood Forest Ecology, Bryology, Lichenology, and Forest Canopy Ecology at Humboldt State University in Arcata, California; Norman R. Pace, director, Pace Laboratory, and professor in the department of Molecular, Cellular, and Developmental Biology at the University of Colorado at Boulder; Marie Antoine, botanist and lecturer at Humboldt State University; hurricane hunters Rebecca J. Almeida, A. Barry Damiano, Albert M. Girimonte, Mark Sweeney, Chuck Rasco; Lori Bast, public affairs and outreach, NOAA Aircraft Operations Center; Jeffrey Masters, Ph.D., and chief meteorologist at the Weather Underground; Roberta Flaherty; Amy Barnes, math teacher, Safety Harbor Middle School; Jennifer Barrentine and Michael Morley; Anestis Diakopoulos, visuals editor, the *Patriot Ledger;* Tom Farrell, chief of interpretation, Wind Cave National Park; Chad Gibson, United States Air Force Reserves hurricane hunter; Eric Banks, undergraduate microbiology research student; Brad Lubbers, Barton Research Group lab technician; lifelong cavers Eric Weaver, Janeen Sharpshair, and Aeron Horton; Lori Rick, director of public relations, MacGillivray Freeman Films; Yvette Reyes, AP Images; Carlsbad Caverns, National Park Service; and cave photographers Dave Bunnell, Rob Coomer, Max Wisshak, Jason Gulley, Phill Round, and Rainer Straub.

I'm especially grateful to Ann Rider, for her insightful editorial guidance and unwavering support through the years; and to Charlie Jackson, whose love cradles each day of this wondrous journey.

"GREAT DEEDS ARE USUALLY WROUGHT AT GREAT RISKS."

—Herodotus, Greek historian (c. 485–c. 425 B.C.)

# HURRICANE HUNTER

**Paul Flaherty:**

**Tracking Dangerous Storms**

# CAVE WOMAN

**Hazel Barton:**

**Mining Microbes**

Some of Paul's favorite gadgets as a child were weather related—including a duck whirligig, which is similar to a weathervane. "When the wind blows, the duck turns into the wind because it's tail-heavy. The faster the wind blows, the faster the duck swings its side arms."

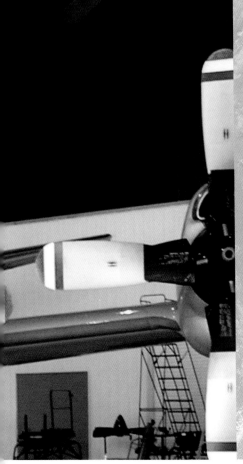

# HURRICANE HUNTER

## Paul Flaherty

### TRACKING DANGEROUS STORMS

Paul Flaherty's head has been in the clouds since second grade. It all started when a Boston TV weatherman named Dick Albert visited his school. "I told him someday I was going to be a meteorologist," says Paul. That's a scientist who studies and forecasts weather.

He meant it. Every chance he could, young Paul hurried home—or to his grandparents' house nearby—to watch the local weather reports. Thunderstorms, heat waves, high winds, thick fog . . . it all fascinated him. "Whenever I saw something, I didn't just think, 'That's kind of neat,'" he says. "I thought, 'How does that happen?' That's really what I was excited about—trying to figure out how things happen and why they happen. The unpredictability of weather was partly what sparked my interest."

Growing up in New England, the budding scientist was particularly inspired by extreme weather conditions. The Blizzard of '78, which blanketed the Boston area with two to four feet of snow in less than a day and a half, "amazed" him. Years later in September 1985, Hurricane Gloria's powerful presence left a lasting impression.

"Being the weather-crazed kid that I was, I remember watching news reports about the storm quite a few days before it made landfall," says Paul. "The Weather Channel had been on the air for three years at the time, and I was always glued to it. I lived about a half-mile from the beach, so everyone wondered if we should be concerned and possibly evacuate the area, but officials deemed it safe to stay."

As Gloria crept her way up the eastern seaboard toward Massachusetts, people stocked up on supplies and prepared for the worst. "My friends and I were excited, because school was canceled for the next day in advance, which meant we had a long weekend," says Paul. "Well, it certainly became a long weekend—a weekend plus a few extra days.

The February Blizzard of '78 buried cars in several feet of snow and stranded motorists for days. It also stirred Paul Flaherty's passion for extreme weather.

"I worked at a local convenience store called PJ's Mini Mart, about two blocks from my house. My bosses—Pete and Jack—were concerned about the area losing power, so they had us make many, many bags of ice." (The ice would help people to keep food fresh if refrigerators stopped working.)

On September 27, Gloria's winds kicked up—reportedly reaching as high as 109 miles per hour in some places. "With the winds came the falling trees," says Paul. Then downed power lines. By midday, dark skies cast an ominous shadow over the area and fueled intermittent rain squalls.

"Although my parents told me not to go, one of my best friends and I headed to Wollaston Beach," says Paul. "I couldn't believe how much stronger the wind was blowing there," he says. "The sand blinded me at times, and it was the first time I saw the ocean crash over the seawall."

What Paul recalls most vividly, however, is the mesmerizing sky. "I was always looking at the clouds," he says, "but I had never seen clouds moving so fast! It was like watching cars go by on the highway . . . When I saw those clouds that day, it was no longer that I wanted to know more about the weather but that I *had* to know more about the weather. At that point, there was no turning back: while meteorology remained my

Paul's interest in meteorology was sparked by a school visit from a Boston TV weatherman. Today, he inspires students—including middle-schooler Michael Morley.

Legendary Daredevils: The first people to fly into the eye of a hurricane did it on a dare. In 1943, U.S. Air Force pilot Joseph Duckworth and navigator Ralph O'Hair took to the stormy skies—without telling anyone—to prove that their single-engine plane could withstand any weather. The pair successfully completed their mission and paved the way for others—including the 53rd Weather Reconnaissance Squadron, now based in Biloxi, Mississippi. These hurricane hunters survey storms in the Atlantic, Caribbean, Gulf of Mexico, and Central Pacific for the National Hurricane Center and have been flying more than sixty years.

interest, tropical storms became my passion. I didn't know then that people could fly into hurricanes."

## STORM SCIENCE

As planned, Paul studied meteorology in college, where he learned about the atmosphere, weather patterns, and climate changes. He worked in a special security unit of the United States Air Force and eventually went on to teach meteorology to military students. One day he spotted a job posting for a hurricane hunter and thought, *Wouldn't it be* amazing *to fly inside a hurricane?*

Today, that's exactly what Paul does for a living—flies into the eye of some of the world's most destructive storms, gathering information about their strength and direction to help keep people safe. The data he collects helps weather forecasters track the path of potentially deadly storms and alert communities through television, radio, and the Internet.

Hurricanes are extreme tropical cyclones—spiraling storms that form over warm seas and rotate counterclockwise. Fueled by heat and moisture, hurricanes pack winds of 74 miles per hour or more, with gusts that can top 200 miles. While each storm varies greatly in size and intensity, hurricanes typically extend more than 300 miles wide and move at 10 to 20 miles per hour. On average, they survive about nine days.

Hurricane hunters—including pilots, navigators, and meteorologists—carefully plan each mission before taking to the air.

Hurricanes that occur west of the International Date Line in the Pacific Ocean are called typhoons, while those that take place in the Indian Ocean are called cyclones.

This satellite image of Hurricane Katrina was taken in the early afternoon on August 28, 2005, by NASA's Terra satellite. At landfall, Katrina's winds topped 125 miles per hour.

A cross section of a hurricane reveals its three primary parts: the eye, or relatively calm center that's typically ten to forty miles long; the eye wall, a towering mass of storm clouds surrounding the eye column that produce violent winds and rains; and rain bands, curved stretches of thunderstorms projecting from the eye that sometimes spawn tornadoes. Moving from the outer edge of a hurricane to its center, you'd first encounter light rain and wind, and then a dry and weak breeze, reverting back to increasingly heavier rain and stronger wind—over and over again—with each period of rainfall and wind becoming longer and more intense toward the eye, say officials at the National Weather Service.

Hurricane hunters such as Paul, who works for the National Oceanic and Atmospheric Administration (NOAA), fly straight through these storm layers into a hurricane's eye. As meteorologist and flight director, Paul leads the crew into the center of a hurricane and determines the safest way to snake through the blinding winds and rains of the eye wall.

How can planes fly in such high winds?

"The plane doesn't always stay so steady," says Paul. But it's not the high winds that cause the problems; it's the wind shear, either vertical or horizontal. Wind shear happens when there's a sudden change in wind speed or direction along a plane's flight path. "So if we fly in a very strong storm but the winds don't increase or decrease rapidly throughout the eye wall, we will have relatively little horizontal shear and it should be a smoother ride." However, when storms have "hot spots" of strong vertical shear—powerful air currents called updrafts and downdrafts—"then the ride could become quite rough." Developing storms usually have the most dangerous drafts, says Paul. "It's my job to keep us out of these areas as best as I can."

To do this, Paul relies on radar equipment and analytical skills gained through years of experience. "I have to keep in mind that the storm is moving and spinning," he says. "So what's directly in front of me on radar, or what's directly in front of the aircraft at the time we're getting close to the storm, may not be what's still in front of me by the time we get there."

NOAA flies two four-engine WP-3D Orion turboprop planes directly into a hurricane's eye. A turboprop engine allows for a near instantaneous response when pilots need to accelerate or decelerate, explains Paul. This is *extremely important* when entering hurricane eye-wall conditions. Turboprop engines are also better equipped to handle a hurricane's powerful precipitation than the typical turbojet engine found in commercial airliners. They're especially designed to limit the amount of water entering the engine, says Paul.

The "P-3" planes—one affectionately nicknamed Kermit the Frog and the other Miss Piggy—feature three types of radar. The

ABOVE: Curved stretches of thunderstorms, called rain bands, project out from the eye of a hurricane. The closer to the eye, the more violent the storms. Note the red areas in the image above, which indicate bands of heavy rain. BELOW: Hurricane hunters for NOAA carve through the eye wall of a hurricane flying in Lockheed WP-3D Orion turboprop planes. The P-3s, which carry a crew of eighteen to twenty people and cruise at 345 miles per hour, allow scientists to collect storm data at altitudes of 1,500 to 25,000 feet. The information helps forecasters track and predict a hurricane's intensity and movements.

Hurricane hunters fly straight through storm layers into the eye of a hurricane. When inside the eye, they're surrounded by a wall of clouds that stretches thousands of feet high and tilts backwards—creating a stadium effect. Above them are blue skies and below, stormy seas.

first is a "typical nose radar. But this only lets you see what's happening in front of you," explains Paul. The second is a special fuselage or "belly" radar that provides a 360-degree horizontal view around the airplane with every "sweep."

"When we're inside the hurricane, I'm able to see not only what's happening in front of us, but what is happening in every direction," says Paul. "This lets me keep an eye on the entire storm at all times, even when it's behind us. Sometimes in a rough storm, the safest way out might be off to the side, or even the way we came in. The belly radar allows me to keep that in mind."

A third type of radar, called a Doppler radar, sits in the plane's tail. Like the belly radar, it sweeps 360 degrees, only vertically. "As we go into a hurricane," says Paul, "the tail radar will let me see the heights of the eye wall, as well as where some of the strongest updrafts may be located. If we are flying through lines of thunderstorms or along a rain band, the tail will give me a lot of great meteorological data. But in the eye of a hurricane, or when approaching the storm, it's the belly radar, primarily, and the nose radar that I'm glued to."

Unlike the P-3 turboprop plane, NOAA's sleek and technically sophisticated Gulfstream-IV jet (shown in front) flies around developing hurricanes instead of through them. Cruising at 530 miles per hour, the G-4 collects data from every level from 45,000 feet down to provide forecasters with a three-dimensional view of steering currents. This information supplements the data collected by the P-3s.

When they're not in the air, hurricane hunter planes are maintained and operated out of NOAA's Aircraft Operations Center at MacDill Air Force Base in Tampa, Florida.

## INTO THE EYE

When the time comes to carve through a hurricane's eye wall, the Fasten Seat Belt light flashes red and the crew prepares for a bumpy ride into the center of the storm. The team—consisting of pilots, navigators, researchers, technicians, and reporters—buckles in and checks for loose items. The potential to get hit pretty hard going in is always there, Paul says. "So we look around and make sure everything is strapped down, and then we hold on and just wait."

After a choppy ride drilling through wind, rain, and turbulence, the plane reaches the hurricane's center. Suddenly, all is calm. In the eye, you are surrounded by a 30,000- to 50,000-foot wall of clouds that tilts backwards and creates a stadium effect, says Paul. "When you look up, you see clear blue skies." If the sun happens to be rising at the time, the views can be spectacular. No time for sightseeing, however. The team's on a mission.

Their goal? To find the "absolute center" of the hurricane and mark it for the National Hurricane Center. The eye is critical to understanding the storm's central air pressure and how it is changing, explains Paul. Air pressure is the weight of the atmosphere—the blanket of air surrounding the earth—pressing down on objects. If the central air pressure drops inside the column of a hurricane's eye, that tells meteorologists that wind speeds will most likely increase, says Paul. "If the pressure rises, winds are expected to weaken."

One way hurricane hunters measure air pressure is by launching a small device called a Global Positioning System (GPS) dropwindsonde from the back of the plane.

Storm Post: During missions, Paul Flaherty operates from the flight director's station in the P-3 (behind the cockpit). The station is equipped with radar displays, two satellite phones, a laptop computer, and various sensors—including one that tells Paul how much water is in the clouds the plane flies through.

20

As the "sonde" floats down through the eye wall and into the sea, it collects data such as pressure, temperature, humidity, wind speed, and wind direction. This information is radioed back to the plane at two Hertz, or twice per second, so meteorologists such as Paul can analyze the data and send it via satellite to the Hurricane Center, as well as to the National Center for Environment Prediction. There, forecasters feed the information into computer models that simulate likely scenarios and allow them to track hurricanes and look for trends: Is the storm losing strength or growing stronger? Has it peaked? When and where will it land?

To provide the most accurate answers, hurricane hunters generally fly through storms several times during their nine-to-ten-hour missions. Flying patterns such as the "figure 4" allows the crew to sample four quadrants of a storm—for example, north, south, east, and west—and "hit the center of the eye twice." In general, forecasters prefer that hurricane hunters make two figure 4s through a storm. "In some cases, we have flown into the eye many more times," says Paul. "With Hurricane Jeanne [September 2004], for example, I flew into the eye twenty-six times over three days."

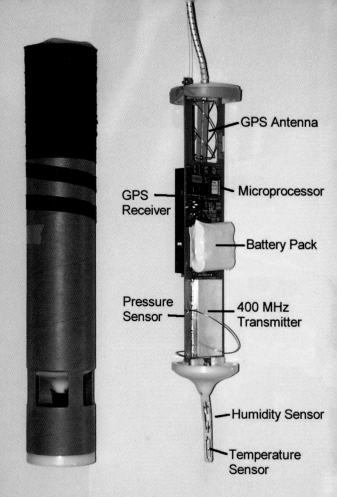

GPS Antenna
GPS Receiver
Microprocessor
Battery Pack
Pressure Sensor
400 MHz Transmitter
Humidity Sensor
Temperature Sensor

ABOVE: Close-up of a dropwindsonde.

## RISKY BUSINESS

While Paul spends much of his time flying through storms during hurricane season, he doesn't consider himself a thrill-seeker. "People think that you must be an adrenaline junkie to do this," he says. "But I just have a passion for

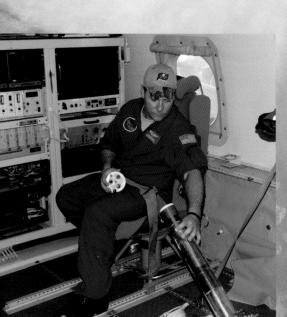

LEFT: Ready to Roll: Electronics technician Chuck Rasco shows how he prepares to launch a GPS dropwindsonde from a chute in the back of a P-3 turboprop plane. The device, which is released in the center of a hurricane's eye, floats down to the sea on a small parachute and collects information such as air pressure and wind speed. Twelve to twenty-four sondes—each costing about six hundred dollars—are dropped during a flight's mission.

the weather. While we're all aware that there's a bit of danger to the job, we try to surround ourselves with the best people. We work as a team to cover each other and to keep it as safe as possible."

In 2003, for example, Paul's plane lost the use of one of its engines while flying through Hurricane Isabel. "The crew did exactly what it was supposed to do to get us back safely," he says. "When something like this happens, we immediately terminate the science mission and head back to base, because flying on three engines instead of four puts more stress on those other engines." The team was lucky that the engine failed just as the plane was heading back toward the storm. "It would have been a lot scarier if we had been inside the eye when it happened, because then we'd have had to find our way out through the eye wall with only three engines—something we really wouldn't want to do."

Others haven't been so fortunate. Jeff Masters, NOAA's flight meteorologist on a mission heading for Hurricane Hugo's eye in September 1989 describes the chilling scene.

## HUNTING HUGO: DISASTER

*"Thick dark clouds suddenly envelop the aircraft. A*

Visual Aid: One of the highlights of the meterologist flight director's station on the P-3 aircraft is a bubble window, such as the one shown, which allows Paul to stick his head outside and look forward, above, and around the plane. "Visual observations are a big part of my job," he says.

*titanic fist of wind, three times the force of gravity, smashes us. I am thrown into the computer console, bounce off, and for one terrifying instant find myself looking DOWN at a precipitous angle at Sean [the navigator] across the aisle from me.*

*"A second massive jolt rocks the aircraft. Gear loosened by the previous turbulence flies about the inside of the aircraft, bouncing off walls, ceiling, and crew members . . . Our 200-pound life raft breaks loose and hurtles into the ceiling . . .*

*"A third terrific blow, almost six times the force of gravity, staggers the airplane. Clip boards, flight bags, and headsets sail past my head as I am hurled into the console. Terrible thundering crashing sounds boom through the cabin; I hear crew members crying out. I scream inwardly. 'This is what it feels like to die in battle . . .' "*

*"The aircraft lurches out of control into a hard right bank. We plunge toward the ocean, our number three engine in flames. Debris hangs from the number four engine.*

*"The turbulence suddenly stops. The clouds part. The darkness lifts. We fall into the eye of Hurricane Hugo . . .*

*"For several eternal terrifying seconds, I watch the massive, white-frothed waves below us grow huge and close. I wait for impact, praying for survival. With two engines damaged, both on the same wing, I know that our odds are not good."*

*The Hurricane Hugo crew miraculously made it out alive that day as pilots pulled the plane out of the dive "a perilous 880 feet from the water." But their fate easily could have gone the way of a handful of other hurricane-hunting specialists who lost their lives flying severe storms.*

UPPER LEFT: Forecasters correctly predicted Hurricane Katrina's path with the help of data collected by hurricane hunters.

BELOW: A satellite image of Katrina from about 22,000 miles above the equator.

RIGHT: A sampling of Katrina's devastation. The damaged home belongs to Paul.

Despite such dangers, the rewards of hurricane hunting far outweigh the risks, says Paul. Hurricane Katrina's devastating effects on the Gulf Coast states of Louisiana, Mississippi, and Alabama in 2005 made that especially clear. "I flew Katrina for five nights starting when it was a tropical storm off Miami," he says. "I sat there and watched as it got closer and closer to the coastal areas where I used to live in Biloxi, Mississippi. When I saw where it had made landfall, I just couldn't believe it."

The day after Katrina struck, Paul surveyed the area. He was "in shock" during the entire damage-assessment flight. "So many of the restaurants that I used to go to were no longer physically there . . . the beach had taken over. So many people that I used to work with and all my friends from the

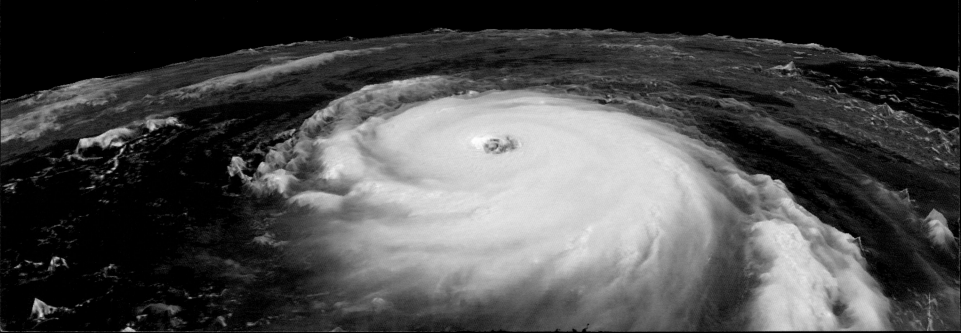

ood where I lived lost everything. The house I built on fourteen feet of water."

aul's friends and neighbors were grateful to escape rath with their lives. Advance warning systems and red directly from the eye of the storm helped save he hundreds of thousands of people who evacuated rly.

part of the reason [people survived] is because we here flying in the storm, doing our job," says Paul. old by the National Hurricane Center that if you run ater] models and remove the data we collected in Katrina, the landfall forecast is off by two hundred loss of life most likely would have been many times t really put an exclamation point for me on why we e do and is the primary reason why I'll be ready to t there each and every season."

# QUICK QUESTIONS
# HURRICANE HUNTER

**Q. Who flies on hurricane hunter missions?**

A. We generally have two pilots and a flight engineer up front on the P-3 hurricane hunter turboprop planes. Right behind them sits the flight director/meteorologist and the navigator. We also have a minimum of three technicians in the back to keep everything running. If anything goes wrong at my station, I call for them.

**Q. Does anyone else ever fly with you?**

A. Yes. We're involved in a variety of worldwide meteorological, oceanographic, and environmental studies, so quite often we'll have scientists on board such as chemists who want to sample the air. We fly with a lot of weather instruments in development for research projects. Many times, these instruments come from universities, and we'll have the students and professors who are working on them fly with us. During hurricane season, we also have quite a bit of TV, newspaper, and radio crews fly along.

**Q. What do you eat on a hurricane-hunting mission?**

A. Everyone usually brings a bag lunch. Most people bring food from the local sub shop. But some bring foods to help settle their stomachs, since we sometimes get bounced around a bit. They might bring a stack of crackers and bread and chew on that the whole flight. Others get a little crazy and may bring along bowls of chili. That's usually the last thing people want to see in the middle of a flight.

**Q. Have storms become stronger and more unpredictable in recent years?**

A. The question is being heavily researched, studied, and debated. If you asked me in December 2005—after the crazy 2004 and 2005 hurricane seasons—my immediate response may have been yes. But as we know, the 2006 and 2007 seasons were relatively mild. At times, it seems a change is happening. And we hear so much about it, we almost think, *It must be true*. But as scientists, we have to look at all the data before reaching a conclusion.

**Q. Hurricane season runs from June 1 to November 30. What do you do when the season ends?**

A. Most people don't realize we fly year-round. Last year, we flew air-pollution studies for six weeks in Houston, Texas. We also had people in St. John's, Newfoundland, who flew storms in the North Atlantic Ocean to help calibrate (adjust) satellites that estimate wind speed. I've also flown out of Costa Rica, where we worked to better understand how tropical storms are formed. In addition, we've flown out of Ireland, Hawaii, and Alaska, where our goal was to improve winter storm forecasting. A few years ago we traveled to southern Illinois to fly severe Midwest storms so forecasters can better predict what triggers them. Called bow echo storms because of their bow-shape appearance on radar displays, these storms can generate tornadoes, flash floods, hurricane-force winds, and massive amounts of lightning. In fact, on my last flight of that mission, we were struck by lightning thirty-four times!

The P-3 planes boast a proud history of service, with a symbol for each hurricane pierced highlighted on its side. Among the more famous hurricanes this plane has flown through are hurricanes Andrew (1992), Katrina (2005), and Felix (2007).

# CAVE WOMAN
## Hazel Barton
### MINING MICROBES

Nichol Creek Cave winds seven miles beneath a sleepy Kentucky mountain. Lush foliage and a fifty-foot rock cliff camouflage its secret, watery entrance. Looking to explore the cave's inner beauty and biology is British-born Hazel Barton, a microbiologist at Northern Kentucky University. Hazel hunts the earth's hidden frontiers—from glacial ice caves in Greenland to underwater caves deep in the jungles of Mexico—for some of its tiniest inhabitants. These single-cell organisms, called microbes, include bacteria and fungi. They live everywhere—from in the air we breathe to inside our bodies—and are considered the oldest form of life on earth.

Some hardy microbes thrive in places never before thought possible, such as searing-hot ocean springs and the bottom of bitter-cold Antarctic lakes. Scientists refer to these super-resilient creatures as "extremophiles." They believe the microbes' ability to flourish under extreme conditions may provide insights to everything from life on Mars to cleaning the environment. Hazel Barton studies extremophiles that

Hazel rappels down a drop in the Pandora's Boxwork area of Black Chasm Cavern, Amador County, California. The cave is noted for its helictites—cave formations that grow as small twisted structures projecting at different angles.

Microbes, such as the bacteria pictured in the background, live everywhere—in the air and in our bodies. Microbes that live in extremely hot, cold, acidic, or starved conditions are called extremophiles.

live in caves—dark, dank environments with little food—and does whatever it takes to reach her cavernous laboratories, from rappelling off vertical cliffs to scuba diving in underwater passageways. "Caves are incredibly starved," says Hazel. "They're sealed off from the surface so there's no photosynthetic energy [sunlight] getting in."

How do cave microbes adapt to such harsh conditions and manage to survive?

Scientists aren't exactly sure, but Hazel thinks the microbes create a community that works together to stay alive. In developing her theory, Hazel collected a sample of cave-dwelling microbes living on a rock and grew, or cultured, them in a laboratory. "We grow most microbes in the lab with about fifteen grams of nutrients," she says. "You know, a couple of packets of sugar. But these microbes live on one-thousandth of one grain of sugar per liter of water, so (the nutrients they need are) tiny, tiny amounts in comparison."

The cave "bugs" also reproduce more slowly than the norm. "If you grow *E. coli* bacteria in the lab, you'll see a colony [a cluster of microorganisms] in sixteen to eighteen hours," explains Hazel. "But with these guys, it may take two or three weeks." When the extremophiles in Hazel's lab finally multiplied, they surprised researchers at the other end of the microscope.

"We thought that we would find two or three species that are very, very good at making a living when there's no energy around," says Hazel. "But we found five hundred species—species that we wouldn't expect to see. Individually,

Hazel Barton and Jason Gulley collect samples of microbes living on rock in Lechuguilla Cave, which is located at Carlsbad Caverns National Park in New Mexico. Lechuguilla Cave is among the longest caves in the world and is the deepest limestone cave in the United States.

30

it didn't make any sense, but when you put them together as a group, you've got organisms that can take energy and nutrients from the air. You've got organisms that can take nutrients and energy from the rock, and you've got organisms that can break down the tiny amounts of energy that are percolating out of soil into the cave.

"Put it all together, and you have a community that gets energy from multiple sources," she says. "It's like Cincinnati. If you had a million people who did one kind of job, the city wouldn't work. But you have people who take the trash, you have people who teach, you have people who bring the food in, sell it, and everybody has his role to make the city function. In caves, the energy levels are so low that you can't make it on your own. But when you're willing to share, there's enough to go around."

Hazel developed her "community-driven" energy hypothesis about cave microbes six years ago and has been researching it ever since. "We're not exactly sure how they work together as of yet," she says. Extremophiles could be sharing byproducts, detoxifying toxic compounds, or turning over nutrients as other bacteria die. These are a few of the possibilities.

"Some people have a hard time accepting there are multiple explanations to what we're seeing," she says. "This is my hypothesis, so I'm testing it. Others have come up with alternative ideas as to how it could be working."

After Hazel collects cave microbes, she grows the bugs in her laboratory by feeding them special nutrients so they'll reproduce and multiply into a colony. Extremophiles grow very slowly compared with other microbes.

## GRAND BEGINNINGS

Hazel's interest in science developed early, with a little help

When Hazel first examined growing extremophiles in her lab, she found what she believes is a community of organisms that work together to stay alive.

from her grandfather. "He was always bringing me chemistry kits, and we would blow things up in the garage," she says. He also encouraged her to read books and to watch a British television series called *Life on Earth*. At the start of every program, host David Attenborough pointed to the millions of animals and plants in the world and how each found its own unique way of surviving. He then went on to share a few of their stories.

It wasn't long before Hazel knew she wanted to become a biologist. She just didn't know what type. "Then when I was fourteen, we did a lesson in biology in which they gave us petri dishes, and we got to brush our hair over them, stick our fingers in, and do all kinds of things and then come back and look at them the next day to see what grew. And something fell out of my hair and landed in the dish. The next day, this gross yellow snotty thing grew, and it was just amazing to me . . . From that point on, I knew I wanted to do microbiology."

Around the same time, the self-described "homebody" took

Hazel's interest in science sparked early with some help from her grandfather. Here (top) she is in his backyard, playing with a popular product back then called "goo." Today, she uses the same material as part of her microbiology labs.
LEFT: Hazel rappels under the "Dragon's Teeth" in Black Chasm Cavern in California.

an outdoor adventure class that included a caving trip. "Until that point, I'd never gone camping or orienteering or done any hiking," she says. While most of her peers were "terrified" during the excursion, she notes, "I was absolutely fascinated."

Through the years, caving became a relaxing hobby for Hazel, providing her with "the ability to explore the unknown and travel to places that no one had ever been before." Still, she kept caving separate from her work. That is, until she joined the lab of Dr. Norman Pace at the University of Colorado at Boulder. A lifelong caver and world-renowned environmental microbiologist, Dr. Pace encouraged Hazel to combine her interests and make caves her living laboratories.

"You always have to do what your heart says," notes Dr. Pace, who continues to collaborate with Hazel on projects. "Microbial organisms basically run the planet. Yet we know very little about them . . . and cave microbiology."

Since then, Hazel has traveled around the world—from Belize to New Zealand and Greece to Guatemala—exploring hundreds of caves and discovering new species. She's been featured in an IMAX movie called *Journey into Amazing Caves*, in which she descends deep into a glacial ice crevasse in Greenland and dives into the treacherous waters beneath

Hazel gazes at the delicate soda straw formations in Hollow Hill Cave, New Zealand. Soda straws are thin, hollow tubes that look like icicles. They form when water seeps into a limestone cave and drips from the ceiling.

Hazel cave dives in the waters of Mexico's Yucatan Peninsula during the filming of the IMAX feature *Journey into Amazing Caves*. Underwater caves offer scientists new opportunities to collect extremophiles—super-resilient microbes—that may one day result in powerful new medicines. The main drawback? Cave diving is as dangerous as it is exciting. A number of divers have died after losing their way in the passageways and running out of oxygen.

In Greenland, Hazel and a team of explorers descended deep into a glacial ice cave during the making of *Journey into Amazing Caves*. Buried beneath layers of blue and white ice—blue representing summer ice and white for winter—lay microorganisms frozen in time and waiting to be thawed back to life. Some of the samples Hazel collected from the wall of an ice cave to examine for extremophiles were chipped from ice estimated to be about two hundred years old.

the rainforests of Mexico. The "rock star" also traveled to Venezuela for an Animal Planet documentary called *The Real Lost World*. There she surveyed caves formed in large part by microbes.

## LIFE ON THE ROCK

Endless questions—and a fascination with harvesting the unknown—draw Hazel to microbes. "People know how cars work, because they build them," she says. "But no one knows how microbes work."

While plants and animals may look different on the surface, they have the same basic chemistry, explains Hazel. "Microbes all look the same, but they do things different chemically. That's why they can live in extreme environments." Microbes also vary more genetically, with 200 million or more species inhabiting our world. This diversity arms them with more problem-solving strategies.

"If something goes wrong and you only have a couple of ways to deal with it, chances are you may not survive," says Hazel. Microbes, though, have multiple options. Some may trade pieces of genetic material called DNA (deoxyribonucleic acid), she says, "or mutate and change their own information and recode it." For example, they may change the function of a protein so it performs under different temperatures.

When fending off rival organisms for food, cave microbes produce poisons to attack their foes. Scientists think certain strains of the toxins may potentially benefit humans by killing bacteria that cause infections. "When some of these species grow, we see little drips of liquid that correspond to antibiotics," says Hazel. One of her goals is to identify and extract these agents so scientists can produce more powerful disease-fighting drugs.

Another objective is to continue to work with NASA (the National Aeronautics and Space Administration) to uncover clues as to how life may exist on other planets. If there's any life on Mars,

for example, it would probably be in the subsurface, says Hazel. "We know that there's volcanic activity on Mars. We know there has been water there in the past and that there's a bit of evidence for present water. And we know that underground, wherever there's water and an energy source, you have a lot of microorganisms." By studying extremophiles and the chemistry of caves on earth, scientists hope to one day make it easier to identify and locate signs of life on other planets.

## BURIED TREASURES

Millions of uncharted caves await exploration beneath the earth's surface. Nichol Creek Cave is a recent discovery, most likely formed a million and a half years ago. It's an epigenic cave, which means it was created by rainwater that seeps through cracks in the soil. As water flows through the fractures, it picks up carbon dioxide, which turns it into a weak carbonic acid—"like Coca-Cola," Hazel says— that eats away at the rock. Over thousands of years, cavities form and gradually grow into channels and passages people can explore.

On a crisp October day, Hazel and her team prepare to journey into Nichol Creek. Before venturing in, they huddle near the cave's entry and double-check their gear and supplies. Helmets, wet suits, boots, gloves, rope, three sources of light, extra batteries, cameras,

Evidence of possible water sources on the planet Mars, such as these gully channels found in a crater, indicates the potential of life.

FAR LEFT: Sometimes the most dangerous part of caving is making it to the cave. Here Hazel (at right) and fellow caver Nancy Aulenbach rappel three hundred feet in 112-degree weather to reach an unexplored cave hidden in Arizona's Grand Canyon.

NEAR RIGHT: Hazel scrapes corrosion residue from a wall in Lechuguilla Cave, New Mexico. The soft material is residue from what had been solid limestone. The corrosion appears to be the work of bacteria eating away at the rock.

Hazel and research student Eric Banks carefully pack lab equipment into a waterproof case before the team heads out to Nichol Creek Cave for the day.

tripods, notebooks, pens, snack bags, and a waterproof case for the lab equipment . . . Ready to go.

Today's mission: to gauge the activity of microbes that have eaten into the cave's rock and measure the conditions they live in, including the humidity and acid levels, to better understand and recreate them in the lab.

One by one, the seven cavers squeeze through the narrow passageway leading several feet to the main cave. For two hours, they slosh forward—often on hands, bellies, and knees—in the "wet" cave before spending another hour hiking on dry land and climbing rocks to their ultimate destination. When the team reaches the testing site, lab technician Brad Lubbers sets up the microprobe equipment under a putty-like substance on the ceiling. Everyone else breaks out the snacks.

"See the rock and how soft it is?" Hazel whispers. "We've done some chemistry on it, and it's calcite [a common mineral and the main component of limestone]. That's what the cave's made of. We think a flood came through and the clay got stuck on the ceiling. When that happened, it stopped water from coming in," she says. "Water's always dripping into the cave, but when it can't come through the clay layer the calcite becomes saturated. When it becomes saturated, it has a lot of moisture and energy in it, and we think the microbes use it to produce an acid." The microbes excrete out the acid in the form of waste after consuming the water, and it's believed this acid eventually turns the rock to mush.

Hazel studied a sample of the soft rock in her lab and found it "absolutely packed with microbes." Next, she shipped it off to NASA. "We sent them a sample to figure

The entrance to Nichol Creek Cave is hidden beneath lush foliage and a fifty-foot rock cliff. Experienced cavers—such as Janeen Sharpshair and her son Aeron Horton, shown here—wear wet suits, boots, and gloves to get them through their first two hours of sloshing underground.

Cave Cricket: Many animals live in caves. Some, called troglobites, adapt to the total darkness and spend their entire lives in caves. Others, such as this cave cricket, which measures about three quarters of an inch, can live in or out of caves. They're referred to as troglophiles.

Popcorn formations, such as those pictured here in South Dakota's Wind Cave, abound in Nichol Creek Cave. Also referred to as cave coral, popcornlike speleothems are made of clusters of the mineral calcite.

out what chemistry the microbes were using, and we think they're using something called methane cycling. There's a constant energy being produced and consumed," she says. "The microbes take energy from the rock, breathe it in, and then breathe out methane. Then another organism, such as methanotroph [a bacteria that uses methane to grow], breathes that in . . . We think that's how they're getting their energy. What makes this unusual is that this would be the first terrestrial, or land, environment where that's been seen. It's usually found deep in the ocean."

Once the equipment's set up, Brad and assistant Eric Banks activate a robot controller that pushes a microprobe into the soft rock about forty times a minute. The probe measures oxygen amounts as well as moisture content. After countless attempts, however, it appears the researchers will have to try again on another trip. The fragile probe used to take measurements breaks each time it's pressed into the rock.

All in a day's work for Hazel. She knows patience and persistence will pay off in discoveries at a later date—in the lab and beneath the earth.

"Going into a cave, pushing and seeing where the cave goes and making the cave go farther than anyone else has made it go—that's man-on-the-moon exploration," says Hazel. Then there are unexpected scientific discoveries: "Like going into a cave that shouldn't exist and seeing things that shouldn't exist . . . such as weird and wonderful formations." You try to figure out why they're there and how they formed, she says. "You hypothesize and test."

Lechuguilla Cave in New Mexico features an array of rare cave formations—including the largest collection of gypsum chandeliers, such as the one Hazel's admiring. Gypsum is a mineral made of calcium and sulfur. Note the tattoo on Hazel's arm. It's a partial map of South Dakota's Wind Cave.

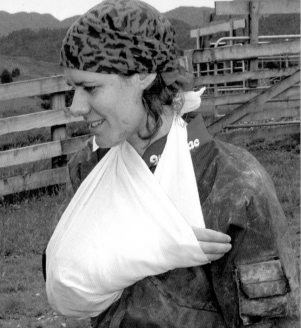

# QUICK QUESTIONS
# CAVE WOMAN

**Q. How does it feel to explore underwater caves?**

A. It feels like flying . . . If you want to go look at something, you kind of kick off, or just glide toward it. Psychologically, it's a lot harder than other types of caving. You have to really be secure in your equipment and know what you're doing. If something goes wrong—such as getting lost or tangled in the line—you only have a couple of minutes to deal with it as opposed to in a regular cave, where you have days before you really start getting into trouble. You can't fool around when you're cave diving.

**Q. Where are the best caves in the world?**

A. France, the United States, and Borneo. It depends what you're looking for . . . Mexico has some great underwater caves.

**Q. What's been your most exciting moment in a cave?**

A. One of the most exciting was the discovery of the Lunatic Fringe Room in Wind Cave in South Dakota. We were doing this exploration, and we were pushing and pushing and pushing, and we found this tiny hole. So we pushed through it, and we got into this room that had a big hole in the floor. We couldn't see a way down, so we came back a month later with a rope. It turned out to be a sixty-foot pit that dropped into a room about the size of a cathedral, lined with crystals.

**Q. Have you ever been caught in a narrow opening?**

A. No. I mean, you don't want to put yourself in that situation—that comes with experience . . . I've certainly crawled into things, and I've thought, "Oomph, it will take a lot of work to get back out." But if you panic, then you get stuck. The trick is to stay relaxed. I've pulled people out who've been trapped, as well as a guy who slipped. He was in a wide crack, and he slipped and fell into a narrower crack. So we had to pull him out, and that took about six hours because he was struggling. When you struggle, you get bigger. So I've never felt trapped in a squeeze. You really don't want to go into something if you don't know whether you can get back out.

**Q. Have you been seriously injured in a cave?**

A. Yes. I was in New Zealand on a photo trip . . . and we were in a stream passage where you could either walk through the passage or climb up to the ceiling and stay dry. Now, photography trips are notorious for being very slow and very long, and you get really, really cold. I didn't want to get wet and cold, so I decided to climb up to the ceiling and stay dry. There was a big boulder in the passage, so we climbed on top of it and then climbed up to the ceiling and traversed. What I didn't know was that there had been a flood in the cave the day before that undermined the rocks underneath and loosened the boulder. So when I stood on it, it went *pheww* and started to move. I jumped and got free, but it gave a blow to my wrist. If I didn't have the caving experience and hadn't jumped as soon as the boulder moved, I would have lost my arm.

FAR LEFT ABOVE: Hazel prepares for an underground camping trip.
FAR LEFT BELOW: She nurses an injured arm received when a boulder broke loose in a New Zealand cave. After surgery and thirty-seven stitches, Hazel soon returned to caving.
RIGHT: Hazel squeezes into a new room discovered in Black Chasm Cave in California.

## Q. What are some of the steps you recommend to keep safe?

A. There are a number of rules that cavers never break, or break at our peril.

• Get the appropriate training: caves are inherently dangerous.

• Wear a helmet.

• Have three sources of light.

• Tell someone where you're going and when you'll be back.

• Wear appropriate clothing for the cave.

• Leave nothing but footprints: everything that goes into a cave must come out—including human waste.

• Take nothing but pictures.

• Kill nothing but time.

For details, visit Hazel Barton's Cave Science website at www.cavescience.com.

LEFT: Hazel examines specimens in her lab.
RIGHT: She descends to Lake Slytherin on the day of its discovery in an area of California's Black Chasm Cavern called the "Chamber of Secrets."

# SKYWALKER

## Stephen Sillett

### SCALING THE REDWOODS

Maples, oaks, white pines. Growing up in south-central Pennsylvania, Steve Sillett climbed these trees and more. Hoisting himself from branch to branch, he reveled in exploring nature from new heights. "I really enjoyed climbing trees as a kid," he says. "I was very interested in watching birds, so I spent a lot of time out in the woods . . . Oftentimes you can get pretty good views of birds from treetops."

Mysterious life forms also flourish atop the branches, and Steve yearned to unlock their secrets. In college, he studied organisms that live in trees. He became fascinated with forest canopies—the thick, leafy coverings formed by clusters of tall-tree crowns. As part of his college research, Steve climbed the tops of tall Douglas fir trees in Oregon and probed the lush tropical rainforests of Costa Rica. "Every forest canopy is an unexplored

Steve Sillett, an ecologist at Humboldt State University in Arcata, California, is the first scientist to climb to the tops of tall redwoods in old-growth forests. His research offers rare insights into a complex community of life high in the sky. Steve's early interest in trees began in his teens. Here (near left) he explores an old-growth forest at age nineteen.

One of Steve Sillett's most surprising discoveries in the redwoods was finding wandering salamanders in the canopies. He met this fine specimen 207 feet above the ground on the main trunk of a 371-foot tree.

world," says Steve, who is a botanist—a biologist who identifies and studies plants. Many of the earth's species—named and unnamed—live in treetops, and "studying canopies helps us fully understand the biological diversity of the planet."

One forest canopy that Steve was the first known scientist to explore is formed by some of the world's tallest living tress: *Sequoia sempervirens*. These green giants live along the coasts of northern California and southern Oregon and can live to be two thousand years old or more. With the loftiest of redwoods standing higher than 375 feet and resting on trunks twenty feet wide and more, many believed that the trees' crowns were barren of life and beyond reach. But Steve uncovered a whole new world of life. Tucked among the clouds, the redwoods' remote forest canopy offers extraordinary insights into an elaborate aerial ecosystem bristling with plants and animals—from ferns and gooseberry bushes to sea birds and pink earthworms.

Among Steve's most remarkable discoveries is "finding wandering salamanders living in the soils high in the crowns of the redwoods." Salamanders need to keep their skins moist, he explains, so they live in tree pockets that hold water such as "rotting chambers inside trunks or in soils built up beneath ferns." The insect-eating amphibians also breed in the canopy. "Most amphibians have an aquatic larvae stage, in which the eggs are laid and then hatch into a swimming tadpole that metamorphoses into the adult," says Steve. "Not true with these wandering salamanders. They hatch with their legs and tail and everything intact . . . They're just little baby salamanders cruising around eating mites."

Another surprise was stumbling across a myriad of trees—"canopy bonsai"—growing on the redwoods. "We found Sitka spruce trees covered in lichens growing

Sometimes squirrels or birds bring seeds into redwoods, and small trees grow on the tall tree. Pictured is a tanbark oak tree sapling growing at 270 feet off the ground.

Among the life forms found atop redwoods are lichens—unique organisms resulting from a symbiotic relationship between a fungus and algae. The lichen pictured, named *Cetraria chlorophylla,* thrives in sunny areas. Steve found this one growing on a redwood branch 355 feet above the ground.

out of the soil accumulations in the tops of redwood trees," says Steve. "We found oak trees and laurel trees . . . woody plants that live up in the crowns of these enormous ancient redwoods. They never get very big—these trees on trees—but the fact they exist and can live for decades is amazing."

Plants and animals thrive on redwoods in part because the trees reiterate—or repeat themselves—at their crown, sprouting new trunks and branches that can support hundreds of pounds of rich canopy soils. (These soils, made of decomposed leaves and debris, accumulate at the base of new redwood trunks over time.) "When a tree's main trunk is damaged, and the leader [the highest shoot] is killed for one reason or another, it has one of two options," explains Steve. The tree can replace it with a single reiterated trunk that would continue growing and result in "a bend or kink where the break and recovery occurred." Or it could replace the leader with multiple trunks, which often happens when the damage is more severe or occurs later in the tree's life. "These reiterated trunks grow like the trees do when they're young, with a vertical main stem and horizontal branches" that fan up and outward, he says. "In some really impressive trees, dozens and dozens of reiterated trunks form a whole dome-shaped upper crown of the tree . . . creating a candelabra effect."

Rich canopy soils accumulate in redwoods over time, allowing plants such as this fern to thrive. The soils, which are made of decomposed foliage and debris, vary in amounts from tree to tree, but some redwoods hold hundreds and hundreds of pounds. These soil mats in the junctures of limbs and trunks act as sponges, catching rain and keeping areas moist for plants and animals.

Old-growth redwoods often reiterate—or repeat themselves—after they've been damaged. New trunks and branches sprout and fan up and outward like the original tree.

## CANOPY CLIMB

It's a long way up into a redwood—and the first step's the most dangerous. "Redwoods are the tallest trees in the world, but they have a very particular kind of structure when they grow in forests," says Steve, a professor at Humboldt State University in Arcata, California. "The big trees don't have branches down low to the ground." Often the trunk's bare for hundreds of feet, with the first sturdy boughs emerging as high up as twenty-five stories.

To gain a solid footing and begin his climb, Steve fires a bolt from a high-powered crossbow over the tree's branches and launches a fishing line that's tied to it. The bolt then drags the fishing line back to the ground, and this is used to haul a rope up, over, and down. After carefully rigging the tree, Steve "jugs" up the redwood's trunk to the crown's base—all the while suspended from a harness so he can tread lightly and avoid injuring the tree's bark.

Going Up: Once a tree is carefully rigged, a climber jugs up its trunk to the base of the crown.

"When you first ascend a tree, you're not quite sure what you've shot your line over," he says. Dead branches can dislodge and fall. So initially, getting to the crown can be risky. "Once you're up in the top, you can reestablish your climbing path through the crown so that you can avoid any hazards that might exist. And these large redwood trees have lots of hazards, because they've been battered by storms over the centuries." Many trees are more than a thousand years old and may have huge, unstable chunks of deadwood—nicknamed widow-makers—that can break loose, Steve says. "You just have to be careful and avoid those places so that they don't fall off on you or anybody on the ground."

Once while climbing a tall redwood, Steve nearly died.

"After shooting my line into the tree with a bow, I ascended the rope," he

After the first climber reaches the crown of this giant sequoia, two others ascend and measure the main trunk's diameter at regular intervals. Whereas the coast redwood is the world's tallest tree, the giant sequoia is the world's most massive tree.

recounts. "When I reached about forty meters above the ground, there was a loud snapping sound and I began to fall." Incidents like these often happen during a first ascent, so at first he wasn't too alarmed. "However," he says, "after falling ten meters, I panicked and let out a scream of terror. Suddenly, at thirty meters above the ground, my fall stopped and I was jerked to a halt on the rope—spinning in space . . . with the sound of my scream ringing in my ears."

As his heart pounded, Steve courageously continued his climb until at seventy meters he reached the limb that had saved his life. "Apparently," he says, "five meters above the limb, my line had passed over a broken branch. When the branch fell, my rope pinned it to the top of the sturdy limb below. Had the branch not become trapped on the limb, the fall surely would have killed me."

## EXTREME EXPLORATIONS

Some redwood journeys last a day, as the scientist stealthfully moves about the branches and "skywalks," or explores a tree's crown while dangling in midair and without touching it. Other missions last longer and require stays in high-rise hammocks called tree boats. Every tree is structurally unique, says Steve—especially in the old-growth forest. "The trees are hundreds and hundreds of years old, and they've got so much character because they've been hammered by lightning and fire and wind and falling neighbors. And they've responded to all these injuries over time."

Many old redwoods, for instance, have survived fires through the centuries, says

Fire caves are dark, shady places. Still, some plants manage to spring to life in them, such as this huckleberry bush.

Steve. "Parts of their crown will burn and if the burn gets into a pocket of decay or where a big limb has fallen off, it can often hollow out a chamber." These chambers—or fire caves—can grow with each new fire, and over a tree's lifetime it may form several, he says. Fire caves are dark, shady places, so few plants grow in them. "Occasionally there will be a shrub, like a huckleberry bush, that's rooted in the cave, but its branches extend out of the mouth of the cave . . . A lot of times you'll see flying squirrel nests in the cave, or you'll see raccoon, owl, or ravens' nests."

An important part of Steve Sillett's work involves mapping trees to learn more about their structure and how they grow. Here he notes the diameter of a reiterated trunk measured by his colleague Cameron Williams.

Steve measures the amount of light available to the leaves in the crown of this redwood that's more than 370 feet tall by using a digital camera on a self-leveling mount.

## MEASURING UP

One important facet of Steve's work involves mapping redwoods to learn more about their structure and how they grow. Despite years of forest research, we still have a great deal to learn about the inner workings of individual trees, says Steve. How does a redwood respond to weather changes and conditions such as droughts? How does the tree use water that it drinks from the soil and absorbs from rain and fog? To help unravel the riddles of a redwood, he and a team of climbers measure a tree by stretching a tape around its main trunk, limbs, branches, and any reiterated trunks they may find. "We map their diameters at different heights through the crown, and then chart their XYZ coordinates [numbers representing a position point] so they can be built in three dimensions on a computer," says Steve. "That computer model can be used to calculate things like wood volume, bark surface, and leaf biomass [the total weight of the leaves]."

If you're studying a radish, it's easy to weigh it or calculate how many leaves it has, notes Steve. "But when you're studying a redwood, how do you know how big it is?" Mapping is a critical step to understanding a tree's dimensions. "Until we know precisely how many leaves a tree has, how much surface area it has, how much wood it has, and how the different branches are sized and distributed in the crown, we're really never going to be able to understand how the tree grows, let alone how much it grows."

Some redwoods spindle toward the sky at surprising heights. In 2006, naturalists Chris Atkins and Michael Taylor discovered a towering titan in a remote valley of

California's Redwood National Park. The two believed it to be the world's tallest living tree. To verify their find, Steve measured the redwood: first by beaming a laser to calculate the tree's height from the ground, and then—the most accurate way—by climbing the redwood and dropping a weighted fiberglass tape from the top.

The result? A record-breaking 379.1 feet. "We were blown away," says Steve, who wants to protect the tree by keeping its location secret. "That tree was four feet taller than the champ before it." Steve expects the soaring redwood to enjoy a long reign as top tree. "I really have a hard time imagining that we're going to dethrone it anytime soon," he says. "I think it will slowly keep growing, an inch or two a year . . . then there might be a drought and its top will die back, and another tree—probably the previous record-

Steve measures the crown of this giant sequoia using ropes and tools that allow him to move much like Spider-Man.

Sensors mounted in trees collect information for scientists, including measurements of light, wind, temperature, humidity, and precipitation. By monitoring the physical conditions around a redwood, called the microclimate, scientists can gain a better understanding of how a tree's environment affects its growth. Here Steve clears debris from a rain gauge.

In September 2006, Steve Sillett climbed, measured, and confirmed the world's tallest living tree at a record-breaking 379.1 feet. Here's a view of its top. "The only evident damage was from a woodpecker," says Steve.

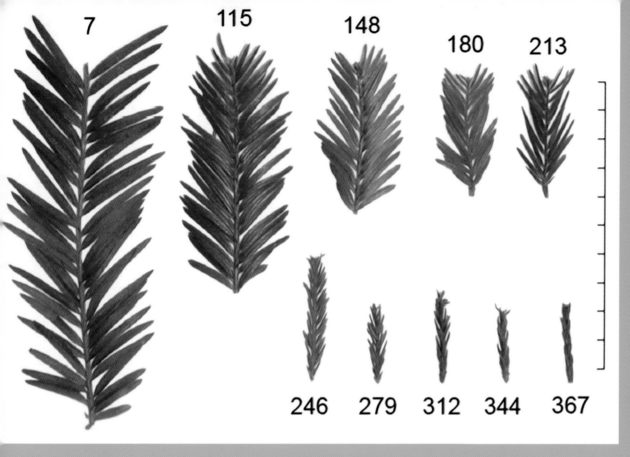

7　115　148　180　213

246　279　312　344　367

Changes at the Top: A redwood's leaves tend to be smaller and scalier higher up in the tree. That's because less water makes it to the upper branches, so redwood leaves become progressively less expanded with increasing height. This shortage of water also ultimately limits how tall the tree can grow. Numbers represent height above the ground in feet.

holder at 375.3 feet—will become the new tallest tree. But we'll see . . . We're keeping track of all the tallest trees. This is important in the face of climate change, pollution, and logging. Right now we have one hundred and fifty trees taller than three hundred and fifty feet, and they're all redwood."

Theoretically, the tallest tree and its counterparts could grow more than 410 feet tall, estimates Steve, who has teamed with several colleagues to study the limits to tree height. After examining many factors, the researchers found that what generally stops redwoods from reaching their maximum potential heights—besides fires, wind, and lightning—is water stress. Redwoods are thirsty trees, says Steve. The tallest grow along streams, in moist, rich soils, and drink hundreds of gallons of water a day. Rain and fog provide some moisture, which is absorbed through the needlelike leaves, he explains. But most of the water trees use to grow comes from their roots—and that water's pulled up all the way through the wood against gravity.

Imagine the water in a redwood flowing inside pipes that connect from the roots and soil to the rest of the tree. As water evaporates from the tree's leaves through tiny pores called stomata, it pulls up more water behind it—slowly but surely moving moisture to the upper crown. But the higher the water has to travel up a tree, the more difficult it becomes to resist the forces of gravity. This can lead to air entering the pipeline and blocking the flow of water, explains Steve. "If this happens a lot, then the top of the tree can't get enough water and may die back." One way a tree works to prevent water loss is to close its stomata. However, since stomata also let carbon dioxide into the leaves, this limits photosynthesis—the chemical process by which the plant produces sugar (food) from carbon dioxide, water, and sunlight.

A redwood's leaves also tend to be smaller and scalier as you move up the tree, says Steve. "All these changes in leaves as a tree grows taller may combine to slow, and eventually stop, its height growth."

## BRANCHING OUT

Studying how redwoods grow is one way scientists such as Steve are deepening our understanding of the earth's tallest trees, which, in recent years, have been dying or showing signs of severe stress. Scientists are assessing the problem and working to find solutions to improve the situation now and for the future. "We're starting to get a real handle on how to gather information at the whole-tree level . . . and to quantify the entire tree," he says. "Once we can do this for a large number of trees—several different species—then we're going to be able to ask some really important questions."

Among those questions: How will climate changes from pollution and global warming affect redwoods and other tall trees? Are the giants versatile enough to withstand the changes? What can people do to reduce the impacts? "I'm concerned

that we don't allow the climate to change so much that the redwood forests decline further," says Steve. "If we lose the tallest trees, future generations won't be able to marvel at the beauty of redwood forests and be truly inspired by the natural world."

For the pioneering professor, such issues propel him personally and professionally.

"You spend hours and hours measuring items in a tree," he says. "You start to learn about the tree—and each tree has its own feel. As you move around through the canopy over time, you see changes that happen to individual trees: 'There's a branch that broke off.' Or, 'Wow, that thing's really grown.' You can actually see changes from year to year in these trees, so it's always interesting to get back into an old friendly tree and see how it has changed and grown . . . It's become such a passion to do scientific work in the forest canopy. If I go without tree climbing for a few weeks, I definitely crave it."

Climbing redwoods takes courage, training, and proper equipment to stay safe. While the work is rewarding and the views are spectacular, if a climber makes one wrong move it could mean his or her life.

# QUICK QUESTIONS
## SKYWALKER

**Q. How long is your typical redwood climb?**

A. It varies from mission to mission. Sometimes we stay aloft for several days and sleep in little hammocks called tree boats. Other times, we just climb all day and come down toward sunset and return the next day.

**Q. What's it like to watch the sunrise from the top of a redwood?**

A. Pretty amazing. You often wake before dawn, because you can hear the birds chirping . . . It's always a little disorienting when you wake up and realize that you are waking up at the top of a redwood.* It kind of heightens your experience. You can peer over the edge of your hammock and look across the tops of the trees into the distance and watch the mist roll in. As the sun rises, there's a breathtaking view of the forest.

*Note: Climbers tie themselves to the trees to keep from rolling out of their hammocks.

Bull Creek in Humboldt Redwoods State Park is home to the world's tallest forest, with more than 100 of the 147 known redwoods taller than 350 feet, notes Steve. Almost every tree in this photo is more than 300 feet tall. "We owe a great debt of gratitude to the Save-the-Redwoods League for helping protect some fine examples of old-growth redwood forest. These forests were nearly destroyed, but there's still a chance to understand them and use this knowledge to restore some of our cut-over [previously logged] landscapes."

**Q. Do you think about the danger when you're climbing?**

A. When I'm climbing to the top of a tall redwood, I'm keenly aware that the ground is hundreds of feet below me. There's a sense that if you make a mistake, you're going to kill yourself. It's very dangerous to climb trees without proper training and without good equipment. I change my main climbing ropes every year. So, yes, there's a sense of risk involved, but you minimize the risks with proper training—which takes months of time, patience, and expert instruction.*

*Note: Steve and his colleagues use an adapted version of tree-climbing techniques that have been developed by arborists, tree surgeons who work with damaged trees.

## Q. How do you avoid hurting a tree when you're in it?

A. Trees are more fragile than people realize. If you run a rope over a branch and hang your weight on it, when you pull the rope back and forth, it literally saws into the bark and can damage the living tissues beneath it—including the inner bark and cambium [the thin layer of cells just beneath the bark]. Your feet also can knock off whole branches along with any ferns, mosses, lichens, and salamanders living there. Soils that build up can be trampled and greatly affected by human traffic, as well. So we always suspend ourselves above the tree surfaces using ropes connected with cambium-savers. We wrap this device around the branch and then run our climbing rope through a pulley on the bottom. This way our ropes do minimal damage to fragile habitats as we move through the canopy. We also never use spikes on our boots, because they can injure the tree with every step.

## Q. Have you had any close calls due to weather?

A. We climb giant sequoias in the Sierra Nevadas (a California mountain range) during the summer, and we've had to retreat hastily out of some trees in lightning storms. That's scary. In the coast redwoods, I once neglected to check the satellite imagery and went to the top of a tall tree in January, and a gale-force winter storm came in suddenly. I was caught at the top in driving hail and freezing rain, so I had to retreat. It was miserable.

**Q. You climb all types of tall trees. How is climbing an Australian eucalyptus tree different from climbing a California redwood?**

A. The only thing that's similar is their height. The Australian species that I study—*Eucalyptus regnans,* also known as mountain ash and swamp gum—sheds its bark every year, so the inner layers are still green. When they're wet, they glow green. And they're slippery, and sketchy, and really weird. They're big, old, windy, nightmarish trees . . . When you get to the top, you can always see the ground. There's never a moment when you can just kind of chill. It's probably the most intimidating tree climbing. At the same time, these trees form one of the most beautiful forests I have ever seen. The canopy is full of life, including raucous cockatoos, gliding possums, and many other amazing animals.

One of the most intimidating tall trees to climb is *Eucalyptus regnans* in Australia, says Steve. It's a flowering tree without a thick leafy crown, "so you can always see the ground." Pictured climbing is Steve's wife, Marie Antoine, who also is a botanist and studies forest canopies. Farther below are their colleagues Jim Spickler (yellow helmet) and Bob Van Pelt (red helmet).

# WANT TO DIG DEEPER?

## PUBLICATIONS

- *Cave Sleuths* (Science on the Edge series) by Laurie Lindop (Twenty-first Century Books, 2006).
- *Coast Redwood: A Natural and Cultural History* edited by John Evarts and Marjorie Popper (Cachuma Press, 2001).
- *Exploring Caves: Journeys into the Earth* by Nancy Holler Aulenbach and Hazel A. Barton with Marfe Ferguson Delano (National Geographic Society, 2001).
- *Hurricane & Tornado* (DK Eyewitness Books) by Jack Challoner (DK Publishing, 2004).
- *Hurricane Force: In the Path of America's Deadliest Storms* (New York Times) by Joseph B. Treaster (Kingfisher, 2007).
- *Taking Science to the Extreme* (Discovery Channel Young Scientist Challenge) by Rosanna Hansen and Sherry Gerstein (Jossey-Bass, 2006).
- *A Voice for the Redwoods* by Loretta Halter and illustrated by Emily du Houx (Polar Bear & Company, 2002).

## DVDS

- *Adventures in Wild California* (IMAX). MMI Image Entertainment, 2001.
- *Hurricane Katrina: The Storm That Drowned a City* (NOVA). WGBH (Boston), 2006.
- *Journey into Amazing Caves.* MacGillivray Freeman Films, 2001.

## WEBSITES

- Cyberflight into the Eye of a Hurricane: www.hurricanehunters.com/cyberflight.html
- Hazel Barton's Cave Science: www.cavescience.com
- Hunting Hugo—meteorologist Jeff Master's chilling story: www.wunderground.com/education/hugo1.asp
- Journey into Amazing Caves: www.amazingcaves.com
- Mammoth Cave—National Park Service: www.nps.gov/maca
- Microbe World: www.microbeworld.org/microbes
- National Hurricane Center: www.nhc.noaa.gov
- National Oceanic and Atmospheric Administration: www.noaa.gov
- Redwood National and State Parks: www.nps.gov/redw
- Save the Redwoods League: www.savetheredwoods.org
- Steve Sillett's Redwood Forest Ecology site: www.humboldt.edu/~sillett

Fourteen-year-old Aeron Horton of Ohio inspects a helictite. He and his parents spend many weekends underground, exploring and mapping new territory.

NOAA flies two hurricane-hunting P-3 planes directly into the eye of hurricanes. One plane is nicknamed Kermit the Frog and the other Miss Piggy.

## HURRICANE HUNTER

**Air pressure:** the weight of the atmosphere pressing down on objects. Generally, high pressure (dense, heavy air) is associated with good weather and low pressure (lighter air) is associated with bad weather.

**Atmosphere:** the mixture of gases between the earth and space.

**Barometer:** a tool for measuring air pressure.

**Dropwindsonde (sonde):** a small device dropped in the center of a hurricane to collect data such as air pressure, temperature, humidity, wind speed, and wind direction. The information helps forecasters track the storm.

**Eye:** the relatively calm, low-pressure center of a hurricane.

**Eye wall:** the ring of storm clouds surrounding the eye or center of a hurricane. The strongest winds and heaviest rains typically occur within the eye wall.

**Figure 4:** two passes made through a hurricane to collect data samples from four quadrants of a storm, such as north, south, east, and west.

**Global Positioning System (GPS) dropwindsonde (sonde):** a weather instrument released in the center of a hurricane's eye to collect information such as temperature, air pressure, and wind speed.

**G-4 or Gulfstream-IV jet:** a high-tech, high-speed aircraft that hurricane hunters fly around developing hurricanes.

**Hurricane:** a type of tropical cyclone—a low-pressure, spiraling storm system that develops in the tropics—with intense winds of seventy-four miles per hour or greater.

**Hurricane hunters:** people who fly into tropical cyclones, such as hurricanes, to collect weather information that will help predict the path of storms and keep the public safe.

**Hurricane season:** the most likely time of year for hurricanes to occur. In the Atlantic Ocean, the Gulf of Mexico, and the Central Pacific Ocean, the hurricane season is June 1 to November 30. In the Eastern Pacific Ocean, it's May 15 to November 30.

**Meteorologist:** a scientist who studies and forecasts weather.

**National Oceanic and Atmospheric Administration (NOAA):** a government agency that studies the earth's oceans and atmosphere and is responsible for tracking and forecasting dangerous weather. Its agencies include the National Weather Center and the National Hurricane Center.

**P-3 or WP-3D Orion turboprop plane:** a type of aircraft hurricane hunters fly directly into storms. The P-3s cruise at 345 miles per hour and allow scientists to collect storm data at altitudes of 1,500 to 25,000 feet.

**Rain bands:** curved stretches of thunderstorms projecting from the eye of a hurricane that sometimes spawn tornadoes.

**Tropical cyclone:** a general term for low-pressure, spiraling storm systems—such as tropical depressions, tropical storms, and hurricanes—that form over tropical waters. In the Northern Hemisphere, winds move counterclockwise. In the Southern Hemisphere, they move clockwise.

**Tropical depression:** a type of tropical cyclone with organized clouds and thunderstorms that have maximum sustained winds of thirty-eight miles or less per hour.

**Tropical storm:** a type of tropical cyclone containing strong thunderstorms and maximum sustained winds of thirty-nine to seventy-three miles per hour.

**Typhoon:** a hurricane that forms in the North Pacific Ocean or the China seas.

**Wind shear:** a sudden change in wind speed or direction—vertically or horizontally—along a plane's flight path.

Brad Lubbers (left) and Eric Banks ham it up before a Kentucky cave expedition. Having fun is always an important part of the journey, they say.

# CAVE WOMAN

**Calcite:** a form of calcium carbonate.

**Calcium carbonate:** a mineral commonly found in rocks such as limestone.

**Carbonic acid:** a weak acid that forms when rainwater mixes with carbon dioxide.

**Cave:** a natural underground chamber or passage large enough for people to enter.

**Caver:** a person who explores caves.

**Column:** a calcite cave formation created when stalactites meet stalagmites.

**DNA (Deoxyribonucleic acid):** a molecule that carries and passes on genetic information.

**Epigenic cave:** a cave created by rainwater that seeps through cracks in the soil, turns into a weak acid, and eats away at the rock over thousands of years until channels and passages form.

**Extremophiles:** microbes that thrive in extreme environments, including those that are extremely hot, cold, or starved.

**Helictites:** cave formations that grow as small twisted structures projecting at different angles.

**Limestone:** rock made mostly of calcium carbonate and generally formed by the accrual of organic remains, such as shells. It's the primary rock found in caves worldwide.

**Microbes:** tiny life forms, such as bacteria, that can be seen only with a microscope.

**Microbiologist:** a scientist who studies microbes.

**Mineral:** an inorganic substance that's not a plant or animal.

**Passage:** a corridor created by water and rockfalls.

**Pit:** a vertical shaft formed by dripping or falling water through a crack.

**Popcorn:** a cave formation shaped like the snack.

**Speleologist:** a person who studies caves.

**Speleothems:** cave formations caused by mineral deposits.

**Stalactite:** a calcite cave formation that hangs down from the ceiling like an icicle.

**Stalagmite:** a calcite cave formation that reaches upward from the cave floor.

**Troglobite:** an animal that lives its entire life in a cave and adapts to total darkness.

**Troglophile:** an animal that can live in or out of a cave.

Some plants—called epiphytes—grow on trees without parasitizing or taking food from them. Redwood forests support a wide variety of epiphytes, such as these lichens and bryophytes (mosslike plants).

**Botanist:** a scientist who identifies and studies plants.

**Cambium:** the living tissue beneath the bark of a tree.

**Canopy bonsai:** small trees that grow at the tops of other trees such as redwoods.

**Canopy soils:** dirt made of decomposed foliage and debris that collects in redwood treetops over hundreds of years.

**Crown:** the upper (top) part of a tree.

**Ecosystem:** interaction of living things, such as plants and animals, within an environment, such as a forest or a tall-tree canopy.

**Epiphytes:** plants that grow on trees without parasitizing or taking food from them. Redwoods support a wide variety of epiphytes.

***Eucalyptus regnans:*** scientific name for the world's tallest flowering plant. Australians call it mountain ash in Victoria and swamp gum in Tasmania.

**Fire caves:** chambers within redwoods and other trees hollowed out by fires over the centuries.

**Forest canopy:** the thick, leafy coverings formed by clusters of tall-tree crowns.

**Laser range finder:** a device for measuring the height of tall trees.

**Leader:** highest shoot on a tree.

**Lichen:** a unique organism resulting from a symbiotic relationship between fungus and algae.

**Mapping:** measuring various parts of a tree so a three-dimensional computer model can be built and provide insights as to how the tree functions.

**Old-growth (ancient) forests:** biologically complex forests that have evolved naturally over hundreds of years.

**Organism:** a life form, such as a plant or animal.

**Photosynthesis:** how green plants chemically make food.

**Reiterations:** new, repeat versions of redwood trees that grow in response to damage to the main trunk.

**Sensors:** tools scientists install on treetops to measure environmental forces affecting trees, including temperature and humidity.

***Sequoia sempervirens:*** scientific name for coast redwood trees—the tallest trees in the world.

**Skywalking:** a tree-climbing method that involves hanging in midair from a complex web of ropes hung on branches and moving about a crown without touching anything.

**Tree boats:** hammocks climbers stretch across branches to sleep in tall trees.

**Widow-makers:** unstable chunks of deadwood within a tree that can break loose and hit climbers as the chunks fall to the ground.

**XYZ coordinates:** three numbers representing a position point that are used to measure and map a tree.

# SOURCE NOTES

## HURRICANE HUNTER

Interviews with Paul Flaherty, meteorologist, flight director, and hurricane hunter for the National Oceanic and Atmospheric Administration (NOAA); and Lieutenant Junior Grade Rebecca J. Almeida. *Hurricanes . . . Unleashing Nature's Fury: A Preparedness Guide* by the U.S. Department of Commerce, the National Oceanic and Atmospheric Administration, and the National Weather Service, revised January 2007. NOAA at www.noaa.gov. National Weather Service at www.nhc.noaa.gov/index.shtml; Hurricane Hunters Association at www.hurricanehunters.com. 403rd Wing, United States Air Force Reserves, at www.403wg.afrc.af.mil. Jeffrey Masters, Ph.D., chief meteorologist at the Weather Underground, www.wunderground.com, and his online account of the near fatal NOAA Hurricane Hugo mission in September 1989.

## CAVE WOMAN

Interviews with Hazel A. Barton, Ph.D., Ashland Endowed Professor of Integrative Science and assistant professor of biological sciences at Northern Kentucky University (NKU), Highland Heights, Kentucky; Dr. Norman R. Pace, director, Pace Laboratory, and professor in the department of Molecular, Cellular and Developmental Biology at the University of Colorado at Boulder; Brad Lubbers, Barton Research Group lab technician; and Eric Banks, undergraduate microbiology research student at NKU. Hazel Barton's Cave Science website at www.cavescience.com. "Combining Microbiology with Other Interests: Hobbies, Holes, and Hollywood," by Hazel Barton, *MicrobeLibrary* article: Focus on Microbiology Education, May 2005. "Cave Slime," by Stephen Hart, *Astrobiology Magazine: Search for Life in the Universe*, June 2003. "Introduction to

An enormous stalagmite called the White Giant catches Hazel's eye as she explores Carlsbad Caverns in New Mexico. Stalagmites, which are created by a buildup of minerals, project upward from a cave's floor.

*Cave and Karst Studies* 68, no. 2 (August 2006): 43–54. *Life on Earth,* natural history television series, British Broadcasting Corporation (BBC One), 1979. *Journey into Amazing Caves,* MacGillivray Freeman Films, at www.amazingcaves.com. "Glossary of Cave Terms" National Park Service, U.S. Department of Interior, Mammoth Cave, at www.nps.gov/archive/maca/learnhome/glossary.htm.

Note: Nichol Creek Cave is a fictitious name given to a real cave in Kentucky that scientists are exploring. Landowners wish to keep the location secret to keep others from exploiting it.

## SKYWALKER

Interview with Prof. Stephen C. Sillett, Kenneth L. Fisher Chair in Redwood Forest Ecology at Humboldt State University, Arcata, California. "Advancing the World's Understanding of Redwood Forest Ecology," website of Prof. Stephen Sillett at www.humboldt.edu/~sillett. "Climbing the Redwoods," by Richard Preston, *The New Yorker,* February 14 and 21, 2005. *The Wild Trees: A Story of Passion and Daring,* by Richard Preston (Random House, 2007). "Higher Learning," by Amy Leinbach Marquis, National Parks Conservation Association, *National Parks* magazine, spring 2006 (www.npca.org/magazine). "One for the Record Books," by Vernon Felton, photos by Kellie Jo Brown, "The Boldt: An Electronic Dispatch for Alumni and Friends of Humboldt State University," May 2007. Save-the-Redwoods League (www.savetheredwoods.org); "Interview: Gorge Koch and Steve Sillett discuss their research on the world's tallest trees," *Talk of the Nation/Science Friday,* National Public Radio, April 23, 2004.

Adapted from the National Weather Service National Hurricane Center Glossary of NHC Terms: www.nhc.noaa.gov/aboutgloss.shtml; *Hurricanes . . . Unleashing Nature's Fury: A Preparedness Guide* by the U.S. Department of Commerce, the National Oceanic and Atmospheric Administration, and the National Weather Service, revised January 2007; and "Glossary of Cave Terms," National Park Service, U.S. Department of Interior, Mammoth Cave, at www.nps.gov/archive/maca/learnhome/glossary.htm.

Hurricane-hunting pilots employ courage and an array of flight instruments to carve through powerful storms.

# INDEX